COUNTRIES
ON THE
WORLD STAGE

SPOTLIGHT ON
Japan

Isaac Kerry

Lerner Publications ◆ Minneapolis

To Lily and Julia

Read by an expert reader.

Lerner Publications Company
An imprint of Lerner Publishing Group, Inc.
241 First Avenue North
Minneapolis, MN 55401 USA

For reading levels and more information, look up this title at www.lernerbooks.com.

Main body text set in Aptifer Sans LT Pro Semibold.
Typeface provided by Linotype AG.

Illustration on page 11 by Laura K. Westlund.

Designer: Athena Currier

Library of Congress Cataloging-in-Publication Data

Names: Kerry, Isaac, author.
Title: Spotlight on Japan / Isaac Kerry.
Description: Minneapolis : Lerner Publications , [2024] | Series: Countries on the world stage | Includes bibliographical references and index. | Audience: Ages 8–12 | Audience: Grades 4–6 | Summary: "Japan is an island nation with a rich history. Learn about the country's formation and current events. Then readers delve into Japan's landscape, economy, and leaders who defined the country"— Provided by publisher.
Identifiers: LCCN 2022049106 | ISBN 9781728492001 (library binding) | ISBN 9798765602560 (paperback) | ISBN 9781728496627 (ebook)
Subjects: LCSH: Japan—Juvenile literature.
Classification: LCC DS806 .K467 2024 | DDC 952—dc23/eng/20221018

LC record available at https://lccn.loc.gov/2022049106

Manufactured in the United States of America
1-53139-51149-1/31/2023

TABLE OF CONTENTS

A New Emperor Is Crowned

IT IS OCTOBER 2019, AND A HISTORIC EVENT IS HAPPENING IN JAPAN. Prince Naruhito stands in front of the imperial throne. He is wearing a burnt-orange robe and holding a wooden scepter—a long, decorated stick. He promises to follow the constitution and unite his nation. The crowd shouts and cheers for the emperor. Naruhito has finished the Ceremony of Accession and becomes the emperor of Japan.

Prince Naruhito participates in a ceremony to become Japan's emperor.

CHAPTER 1

Japan through the Ages

Historians believe people first came to the islands of Japan sometime around ten thousand to thirty thousand years ago. These early humans used land bridges from mainland Asia to come to the islands.

Over the next several thousand years, the people of Japan settled in communities. They shifted from hunting and gathering to farming. Eventually, the people of the islands began to form groups known as clans. From 250 to

神武天皇

Emperor Jimmu is the legendary first emperor of Japan.

710 CE, the Yamato clan grew more powerful than other clans. The Yamato clan eventually took over many of its neighboring clans. They controlled over half of Japan.

The Yamato clan became the major force in Japan. They sent trade and diplomatic missions to China. They created the Imperial Court and the ruling emperor. The court set up the early political system of the nation. The modern Japanese imperial family can trace their ancestry back to these early rulers.

The early Japanese state went through many years of internal wars and power struggles. Eventually, a strong, centralized state was formed around the year 700 CE. However, it would take several hundred years for what we

Serving from 1867 to 1912, Emperor Meiji helped modernize Japan.

THE TOKUGAWA ERA

From 1639 to 1853, the Tokugawa era in Japan limited trading. The Dutch were allowed to trade in southern Japan. Japan also had diplomatic and economic relationships with China and Korea. The Tokugawa shogunate expanded Japan's influence to nearby kingdoms. The current Okinawa region used to be ruled by the Ryūkyū kingdom. Overall, the shogunate controlled the traffic of people and the type of trade. This tight control ended in 1853, when the US government sent a fleet of ships to Japan to threaten them to open up.

consider the modern Japanese nation-state to form. This happened in 1868 with the start of the Meiji Restoration. This project modernized Japan and made it as powerful as other major nations.

Over the years, Japan has developed into a powerful force in the Asian world. It fought successful wars against China and conquered Korea, officially annexing it in 1910. Japanese control of Korea was extremely harsh. The Japanese government banned the use of Korean language in public and destroyed many important historic sites.

Japan joined World War 1 (1914–1918) and fought on the side of the Allies in 1914. It mostly fought German territories in Asia.

CHAPTER 2

The Land of the Rising Sun

Japan is made up of 6,852 islands, although people only live on around 430 of the islands. Japan's main islands are Hokkaido, Honshu, Kyushu, and Shikoku. Together the islands cover 145,937 square miles (377,976 sq. km). Japan is the sixty-third-largest country in the world.

CHINA

RUSSIA

Sea of Okhotsk

Hokkaido

Sea of Japan

NORTH
KOREA

SOUTH
KOREA

JAPAN

北

Tokyo

Honshu

NORTH PACIFIC OCEAN

Shikoku

Kyushu

★ Country capital
International border
Mountains
北 North (compass)

*Philippine
Sea*

ARCTIC OCEAN

NORTH AMERICA

EUROPE

ASIA

ATLANTIC OCEAN

JAPAN

AFRICA

PACIFIC OCEAN

SOUTH AMERICA

INDIAN OCEAN

PACIFIC OCEAN

AUSTRALIA

PACIFIC OCEAN

SOUTHERN OCEAN

Miles

0   50   100   150

0   100   200

Kilometers

Japan is mountainous, so many farmers use terraces to grow crops such as rice.

More than 80 percent of Japan is mountains. Many of these mountains are volcanic. With 440 volcanos, Japan is the second most volcanic country. Underground volcanic activity has led to many earthquakes.

As an island nation, Japan shares no physical borders with other countries. However, it shares maritime borders with China, North and South Korea, Russia, Taiwan, the Philippines, and a United States territory.

Tokyo is the most populous city in the world.

As of 2022, Japan had a population of over 125 million people. It's the eleventh largest country by population. Almost 92 percent of Japanese people live in cities.

Tokyo is the capital of Japan. Over 37 million people live there and in the surrounding area. This makes it the largest urban area in the world. Almost 30 percent of Japan's population lives in Tokyo. Other major cities include Osaka, Nagoya, and Kyoto.

Almost 98 percent of the population are native Japanese. About 2 percent is mainly made up of people from China, Korea, Vietnam, the Philippines, and Brazil. The official language of Japan is Japanese, although other languages

JAPAN'S INDIGENOUS PEOPLES

The people on the island of Okinawa were annexed by Japan in the thirteenth century. They form Japan's largest group of Indigenous people, although the Japanese government does not recognize them as such. Okinawan activists are working to gain recognition as Indigenous people and to remove American military bases from their island. Another group of Indigenous people, the Ainu, are seeking to gain similar recognition.

An Okinawan woman wears a kimono and plays a sanshin.

are spoken, especially by Japan's Indigenous peoples. Some of the major religions in Japan are Shinto, Buddhism, and Christianity. Shinto developed on the Japanese islands, while the other religions were brought to Japan through the Korean peninsula or missionaries.

CHAPTER 3

Rising from the Ashes

Japan has the third-largest economy in the world, behind the United States and China. This is despite the damage the country experienced during World War II (1939–1945).

Tensions that led to World War II started earlier in Asia than in Europe. A major invasion happened in northeast China in 1931. Ten years later, Japan attacked the US naval base in Pearl Harbor, Hawaii. The Japanese military was in control of the country, and they wanted to expand the boundaries of Japan's empire. By joining the Axis powers of

Germany and Italy, the military politicians in Japan wanted control in the Asia-Pacific area.

The war quickly went poorly for Japan and their allies in Europe. Allied bombing severely damaged many Japanese cities and other areas in its empire. The war ended with the catastrophic nuclear bombing of Hiroshima and Nagasaki by the United States, which killed over two hundred thousand people.

A museum destroyed during the bombing in Hiroshima in 1945

Japan's decision to go to war ultimately ended up being devastating for the country. The war resulted in the deaths of around three million Japanese people. The effects of the war wiped out thirty years of economic growth.

As part of the surrender agreement, the Allies, especially the US, took control of Japan. The emperor was stripped of power, a new constitution was created, and several new laws were made.

After World War II, Japan had to rebuild. By 1956 the Japanese economy was bigger than it had been before World War II. In the 1960s, Japan was known for its thriving economy. By 1991 it was larger than the United Kingdom's economy and 85 percent as big as that of the United States.

Economists have several ideas about how Japan did this. One idea is that before World War II, many people in Japan worked on farms. Post war changes in the legal system made it easier for people to move to cities and leave their farms behind. This gave developing industries a new labor force.

Another idea is that during the war, the government created programs that matched people to jobs. These programs continued after the war and helped people find work.

In modern times, Japan has many major industries including car manufacturing. Japan is the third-largest car manufacturer in the world.

JAPAN AND VIDEO GAMES

One of the most popular forms of modern entertainment, video games, owes much of its popularity to Japan. Some of the world's biggest video game companies were founded in Japan, such as Nintendo, Sony, Capcom, and Sega. Video games are incredibly popular in Japan, and the country influences the entire industry.

Shigeru Miyamoto created many of Nintendo's most popular video games.

Only about 12 percent of Japan's land can be used for farming. Japanese farmers use a terrace system to get the most out of their land. They create a series of steps on the country's many steep hills. This allows the country's farmers to grow more crops. The major crop in Japan is rice.

CHAPTER 4

Becoming a Democracy

Japan's current system of government comes from the 1947 constitution that was written with a lot of influence from Allied officers after World War II. It sets the country up as a democracy and has a clause in it that prevents Japan from starting a war.

Japan's government is separated into the legislative, executive, and judicial branches. A prime minister leads the executive branch. The legislative branch has two chambers, the House of Representatives and the House of Councillors. The court system is headed by a fifteen-justice Supreme Court.

The Japanese islands are split into forty-seven different districts called prefectures. These prefectures are similar to states in the US, but they are not as independent.

The emperor of Japan used to rule over the entire nation. After World War II, the emperor lost much of that power. The emperor is a symbol of the nation.

A replica of Japan's constitution

Emperor Hirohito is also called Emperor Shōwa. Shōwa means "bright peace" or "enlightened harmony."

Emperor Hirohito was emperor of Japan from 1926 to 1989. This makes his reign the longest in history. He oversaw an incredibly important period in Japanese history. Beginning in the 1930s, Japan's military became aggressive. Historians are uncertain how much Hirohito was involved in the military's wars. Some think he was opposed to the wars, while others believe he supported them. One of his most important decisions was to surrender at the end of World War II. Many members of the military wanted an all-out defense of Japan. Hirohito ultimately overruled them and surrendered, most likely saving thousands of lives.

A NEW LEADER

In October 2021, Fumio Kishida became prime minister of Japan shortly after he led his party to victory in that year's election. Before taking his new office, he had served as the nation's foreign minister. Kishida is from Hiroshima and opposes nuclear weapons. He oversaw US president Barack Obama's visit to Hiroshima. This was the first time a sitting US president had visited the bomb site.

Shigeru Yoshida was the prime minister of Japan for most of 1946 to 1954. During the war he was arrested by military police for urging the government to negotiate peace. After becoming prime minister, he oversaw the rebuilding of his country. He also signed the final peace treaty with the United States. Historians credit him with setting the path for Japan to become a successful democracy.

Japan's longest-serving prime minister was Shinzo Abe. He was prime minister from 2006 to 2007 and again from 2012 to 2020. Abe sought to boost Japan's economy and was aggressive in his stance toward China. His opponents criticized his refusal to apologize for some of Japan's past crimes, especially involving World War II. Abe was assassinated in 2022 while campaigning.

Japan in the Twenty-First Century

OVER THE CENTURIES, JAPAN HAS GROWN INTO ONE OF THE MOST POWERFUL AND IMPORTANT COUNTRIES IN ASIA AND THE WORLD. However, Japan is facing a number of challenges as it moves farther into the twenty-first century.

Japanese economic growth has slowed down significantly since the 1990s. A major reason for this is the country's reduced birth rate. The population of Japan fell by over six hundred thousand people from 2021 to 2022. Japan has strict immigration laws, so it can be difficult to move there. About 2.5 percent of Japan's workforce comes from other countries. Japan's immigration policy is quickly changing.

While Japan's economic growth is slowing down, car manufacturing remains an important part of the country's economy.

With a life expectancy of about eighty-five years, Japan has one of the highest life expectancy rankings in the world.

Japan has a high life expectancy, which is often a sign of a healthy population. However, it means the government needs to spend more on assistance programs for older adults. Taking care of citizens in this way is an important job for a nation. But it costs more money each year to take care of Japan's aging population. This has put the country into more debt.

Japan has long-running tensions with its neighbor China. Some of these tensions are around economic competition. Japan and China also disagree about borders, especially about how to share the stretch of sea between them. Both countries claim to own 200 miles (322 km) off their coasts, but the actual distance between them is only 360 miles (579 km). This overlap has created several disputes about islands and natural resources.

Japan is one of the most powerful nations in the world. The country has had many successes, but it also faces challenges. How it deals with these challenges will shape the world.

People celebrate the new emperor on February 11, 2020.

TIMELINE

About 30,000–10,000 BCE
The first peoples from mainland Asia come to the Japanese islands.

250–710 CE The Yamato clan begins to grow in power and centralize control.

1543 Portuguese missionaries arrive in Japan as the first Europeans in the country.

1639–1853 The policy of Sakoku stops almost all foreigners from entering the country.

1868 The Meiji Restoration declares Japan a nation-state.

1910 Japan annexes Korea. Korea remains in Japanese control until 1945.

1914 Japan enters World War I (1914–1918) on the Allied side. It attacks German-controlled areas of China.

1941 Japan enters World War II (1939–1945) with an attack on the US naval base at Pearl Harbor.

1945 Emperor Hirohito surrenders to the Allies after the United States' nuclear bombing of Hiroshima and Nagasaki.

1951 The Allied occupation of Japan ends with the signing of the San Francisco Peace Treaty.

2021 Fumio Kishida becomes the prime minister of Japan.

JAPAN FAST FACTS

Name: Japan

Population: 125,816,000

Land area: 145,937 square miles (377,976 sq. km)

Largest city: Tokyo

Form of government: constitutional monarchy

Official language: Japanese

Flag:

GLOSSARY

annex: to take land that belongs to a country and make it part of a different country

constitution: a document that establishes the basic beliefs and laws of a nation, establishes the powers and duties of the government, and outlines the rights of people living there

democracy: a form of government in which people choose leaders by voting

economy: the process or system by which goods and services are made, sold, and bought in a country

foreign: located outside a particular place or country

manufacturer: a maker of products

population: the number of people who live in a place

shogunate: the military government that ruled Japan until the revolution of 1867–1868

surrender: to agree to stop fighting

LEARN MORE

Britannica Kids: Japan
https://kids.britannica.com/kids/article/Japan/345715

Doeden, Matt. *Travel to Japan*. Minneapolis: Lerner Publications, 2022.

Kiddle: Japan Facts for Kids
https://kids.kiddle.co/Japan

Kids World Travel Guide: Japan Facts
https://www.kids-world-travel-guide.com/japan-facts.html

Kissock, Heather. *Tokyo*. New York: AV2, 2022.

Mattern, Joanne. *Japan*. New York: Cavendish Square, 2019.

National Geographic Kids: Japan
https://kids.nationalgeographic.com/geography/countries/article/japan

Van, R. L. *Japan*. Minneapolis: Abdo, 2023.

INDEX

PHOTO ACKNOWLEDGMENTS

Image credits: AP Photo/Pool/Albert Nieboer/picture-alliance/dpa, p. 5; MeijiShowa/Alamy Stock Photo, p. 7; Rapp Halour/Alamy Stock Photo, p. 8; LKW/ Independent Picture Service, p. 10; Jason Arney/Getty Images, p. 12; Jaeyun Jang/ EyeEm/Getty Images, p. 13; d3sign/Getty Images, p. 14; petesphotography/Getty Images, p. 15; Everett Collection/Shutterstock, p. 17; Christian Petersen/Getty Images, p. 19; REUTERS/Alamy Stock Photo, p. 21; Underwood Archives/Getty Images, p. 22; StudioByTheSea/Shutterstock, p. 25; Kei Uesugi/Getty Images, p. 26; Uino/Shutterstock, p. 27.

Cover: Stefan Cristian Cioata/Getty Images.